The Lost Railways of Yorkshire's West Riding:
The Central Section
Bradford, Halifax, Huddersfield, Leeds, Wakefield

Neil Burgess

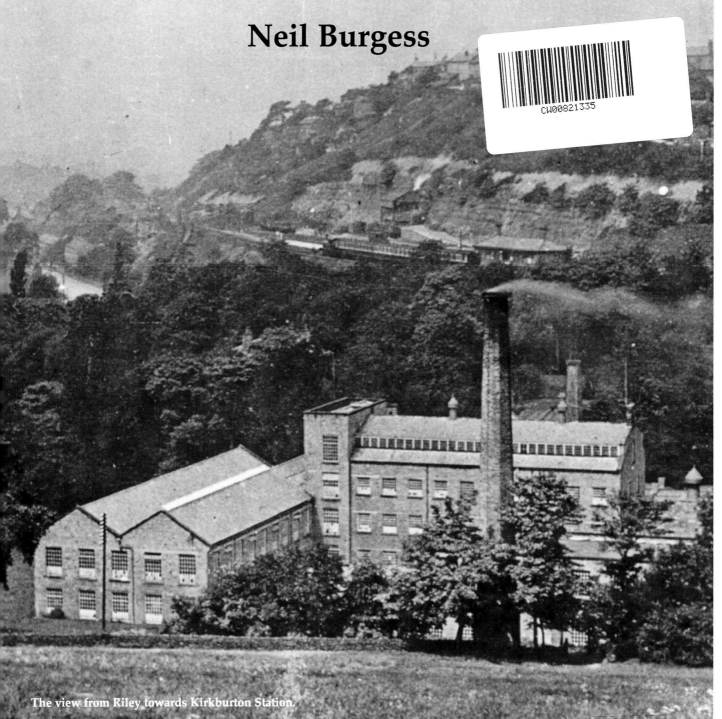

The view from Riley towards Kirkburton Station.

© 2014 Neil Burgess
First Published in the United Kingdom, 2014
Stenlake Publishing Limited
54-58 Mill Square, Catrine, KA5 6RD
www.stenlake.co.uk

ISBN 9781840336573

Kirkstall Station, *c.* 1910.

Acknowledgements

I continue to be indebted to my friend and fellow railway historian Richard Morton for his help in checking and proof reading the main text. His assistance in the preparation of this book is greatly appreciated.

The publishers wish to thank the following for contributing photographs to this book: John Alsop for the front and back covers, also the inside front cover (lower) and inside back cover (upper) as well as pages 1, 2, 4, 5, 6 (both), 7 (both), 8 (both), 9, 10 (both), 14, 17, 18 (both), 20, 22, 23 (both), 24, 26, 27, 28, 29 (lower), 31 (both), 32, 34 (upper), 36 (both), 37 (both), 40 (lower), 41 (upper), 42 (upper), 43 (upper), 44 (both), 48, 49, 51 (lower), 52 (both), 53 (upper), 54, 55, 56, 57 (upper), 58 (both), 59, 60, 62, 64, 66, 67 (both), 68, 69 (both), 70 (both), 72, 74 (lower), 75 (both), 76, 78 (both), 79 (both), 80, 82 (both), 83, 84 (both), 85, 86 (both), 87 (both), 88, 89 (both), 90 (both), 91, 92, 93 (both), 94, 95, and 96 (both); and to Richard Casserley for the inside back cover (lower) and pages 11 (both), 12, 16 (upper), 19 (lower), 21 (both), 29 (upper), 30 (both), 33, 34 (lower), 35, 40 (upper), 41 (lower), 42 (lower), 45, 46, 47, 50, 51 (upper), 53 (lower), 57 (lower), 61, 63, 71, and 74 (upper).

Closure Dates

This book lists dates when stations and lines were closed to regular scheduled passenger traffic. Readers need to recognise that sources vary in deciding closure dates, some giving the last day on which regular services operated, others the first day when closure was effected and no passenger traffic operated. Especially on lines with no regular Sunday service, this might yield a discrepancy of two days depending on the method used. In some cases, particularly before the mid-1960s, stations along closed lines might be left substantially intact and periodically excursion trains called to pick up or set down passengers. In some areas unadvertised workmen's services were also run. Where sources indicate that this happened it may be noted in the text, but it does not affect the official closure date.

INTRODUCTION

If Manchester was the Victorian 'Cottonopolis', then this part of the West Riding was the nineteenth century capital of the woollen trade, the very names of Bradford, Batley, Huddersfield and Halifax summoning up images of 'dark satanic mills' spinning yarn and weaving cloth. Indeed, to many people without close acquaintance with the county – particularly those living in southern climes – the West Riding *is* Yorkshire, the embodiment of everything they associate with 'up north'.

This area of the West Riding was one of the parts of Britain most marked by the industrial revolution, starting in the mid to late eighteenth century and continuing until well after the Second World War. The abundance first of water power and later coal made it a natural centre for manufacturing of all kinds, factories springing up at an alarming rate as towns grew beyond recognition in the years after Waterloo. By the end of the nineteenth century it was reckoned that a quarter of the entire population of England lived in Lancashire and Yorkshire, and most of the white rose county's share was in the West Riding.

The combination of population and industry required transport. Canals came first, but were constrained by the terrain and so gave place to steam-worked railways when these appeared in the 1830s. However, the geography of the West Riding was not particularly conducive to railway-building in many places, certainly once the valley floors had been used up for main routes. As with so many places, the early lines took advantage of the most favourable routes and these, on the whole, have survived best into the modern age. Latecomers tended to be forced to take up the less attractive routes and required heavy civil engineering in the form of viaducts, tunnels and cuttings to get to their destinations.

The concentrations of population conspired to make the electric street tramway and later the motor bus a more attractive option for short journeys and this spelt the beginning of the end for many of the branch lines, often only a few decades after they opened.

Railway companies were keen to build in the area, seeing prospects of healthy returns from the carriage of goods and passengers. The London & North Western, Lancashire & Yorkshire, Midland and Great Central companies all established a significant presence, while the Great Northern invested millions of pounds in creating an empire of lines around Leeds and Bradford. In the east the ancient North Eastern and its upstart rival, the Hull & Barnsley, both made their presences felt. Leeds saw trains from all of them, which must have offered an almost unrivalled spectacle of colour and variety to the 'railwayac' of the early twentieth century. The area also contained some notable minor companies, among them the Middleton Railway in Leeds, reputedly the first public railway – as against a line purely to serve a private undertaking such as a colliery – in the world. The Middleton is now a tourist line, though it certainly has continued to carry goods traffic in its preserved state.

Elsewhere the railway network shrunk as the industries which promoted and sustained it declined or vanished and people turned to cars for daily transport. While this has long been a trend throughout Britain, the area's railways included a good number of minor lines which must have been only marginally economic for much of their existence, not aided by the considerable civil engineering which can hardly have kept down running costs. Most of the Great Northern's network has gone completely, as have whole companies like the Hull & Barnsley. Elsewhere there has been considerable rationalisation.

However, the tide of decline has also turned in some places where it has become clear that the freedom promised by car ownership is in inverse relation to the number of vehicles on the road. The East Coast main line electric network has extended to Leeds and other routes have received a new lease of life as alternatives to increasingly congested roads. The creation of the West Yorkshire Passenger Transport Executive during the 1970s was a step towards an integrated public transport policy for the area and ensuring proper investment. Through the vagaries of the last forty years this remains an important initiative and will hopefully secure the future of railways for many years to come. Whether people see trains simply as a convenient way of getting to a destination, or travel on them with an eye to their history and the struggles which created and sustained them, there is still much to see and travel over in the West Riding.

Long may it continue!

Batley — Birstal

Passenger service withdrawn   1 January 1917 *
Distance   1 $\frac{3}{4}$ miles
Company   London & North Western Railway

Stations closed	*Date of closure*
Carlinghow	1 January 1917
Birstall **	1 January 1917
Birstall Town ***	1 August 1951

* Some sources quote 1916, possibly 31 December.
** Originally named Birstal until 1 April 1907.
*** Originally named Upper Birstal until renamed Upper Birtsall on 1 April 1907.
Renamed Birstall Town on 8 July 1935.

For a town of its size and commercial significance, Bradford was relatively late in being connected to the national railway network, the Lancashire & Yorkshire achieving this with their line from the Spen Valley via Bowling, which entered the terminus at Bradford Exchange in May 1850. The Midland and the Great Northern also served the town in due course but the London & North Western also unsuccessfully sought a route from their Leeds — Dewsbury main line. The section to Birstall was opened in 1852, bringing the company to within six miles of the centre of Bradford but attempts to close the gap proved unsuccessful and this was as close as the London & North Western got to their erstwhile goal.

Passenger services, known locally as 'the Coddy', were generous during the nineteenth century, seventeen return journeys being offered at one time, but the electric street tramway proved the undoing of this line, as with so many of its neighbours. There was also a station at Upper Birstall on the Leeds New Line and this more or less sealed the fate of the line as a passenger route, services ending as a wartime economy in 1917 and never being reinstated. Goods traffic continued for almost half a century more, finally ending on 16 June 1952 with an enthusiasts' special conveyed in a train of brake vans. Part of the trackbed remains as a cycleway.

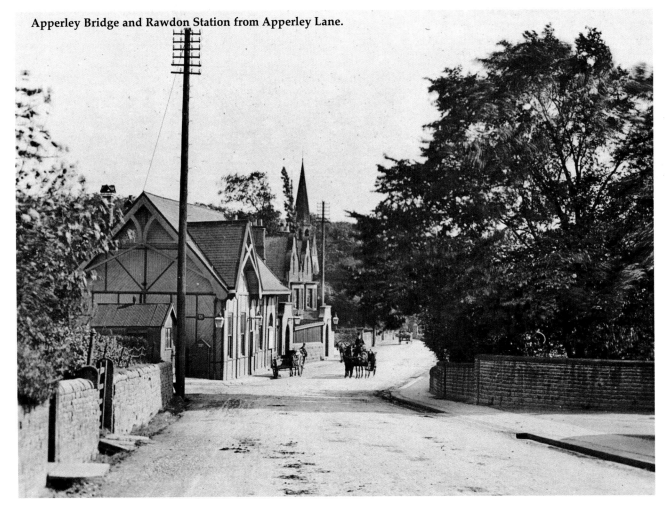

Apperley Bridge and Rawdon Station from Apperley Lane.

Batley — Dewsbury — Ossett

Passenger service withdrawn	7 September 1964
Distance	4 miles
Company	Great Northern Railway

Stations closed	*Date of closure*
Batley Carr	6 March 1950
Dewsbury (first station) *	15 March 1880
Dewsbury Central **	7 September 1964
Earlsheaton	8 June 1953

* Replaced by the second Dewsbury Station when the line was extended.
** Originally named Dewsbury until January 1951.

This short section of line was a loop off the route from Wakefield to Drighlington through Batley, built in order to provide the Great Northern with access to Dewsbury in competition to the London & North Western. Construction commenced from the south, diverging from the main route at Runtlings Lane Junction to the west of Ossett, and the line opened as far as Dewsbury in 1874. The extension beyond Dewsbury to Batley was affected by the trade depression of the late 1870s and it was 1880 before it was completed, along with a permanent station in Dewsbury.

As construction proceeded there were a series of local campaigns to encourage the Great Northern to construct a line to Cleckheaton from Batley Carr, just north of Dewsbury. The bill for the line was rejected by Parliament, but the root of the proposal was dissatisfaction with the Lancashire & Yorkshire's provision and the agitation for the Great Northern to act was such that the Lancashire & Yorkshire agreed to improve matters in partnership with the Great Northern. One consequence of this new-found amicability was the construction of a link between the two companies' stations in Dewsbury to allow a circular service from Leeds via Pudsey, Cleckheaton and Batley to be introduced.

By the first decade of the twentieth century Dewsbury was served by four railway companies, the London & North Western, the Lancashire & Yorkshire, the Great Northern and, after 1906, the Midland – though the newcomer provided goods services only. After the Great War rationalisation was needed and the Lancashire & Yorkshire station at Market Place was closed from 1930. The Great Northern's route survived until 1964, though Batley Carr and Earlsheaton both closed during the early 1950s.

The Great Northern's Dewsbury Station, *c.* **1905.**

Dewsbury Station, with a local train at the platform.

Earlsheaton Station, *c.* 1910.

Batley — Leeds via Tingley

Passenger service withdrawn	2 March 1955
Distance	8 ¹/₄ miles
Company	Great Northern Railway

Stations closed	*Date of closure*
Woodkirk	25 September 1939
Tingley	1 February 1954
Beeston	2 March 1955
Holbeck High Level *	7 July 1958

* Originally named Holbeck until 2 March 1951.

This short line was a further link in the Great Northern's fiefdom around Leeds and Bradford, linking Batley with the 1857 route into Leeds at Beeston Junction, crossing the route from Wakefield to Drighlington at Tingley. The line was constructed at the cost of some heavy civil engineering and opened in 1890, late in the age of railway building.

This piece of the West Riding jigsaw permitted a number of circular passenger workings, a useful way of obtaining as economical a method of operation and rolling stock utilisation as could be envisaged. From opening, the line was served by trains from Leeds running via Ardsley, Dewsbury, Batley and Tingley before returning to their point of origin. Three trains a day in each direction traversed the route – a kind of Yorkshire equivalent of London's Circle Line – until curtailed by the outbreak of war in 1939. A second circular route, this time operated in conjunction with the Lancashire & Yorkshire Railway, which was duly chastened by the threat to its interests by the abortive Great Northern line to Cleckheaton. This ran from Leeds through Tingley, Batley, Dewsbury, the Lancashire & Yorkshire's Spen Valley line, Low Moor (often described as one of the bleakest stations on the system), and then returned to Leeds through Pudsey. No doubt the 'railwayac' of the time would have been fascinated by such a working, but the outbreak of the Great War saw it suspended, never to be reinstated. Road transport undermined the viability of the route and passenger and goods services ceased in 1953.

Woodkirk Station, *c.* 1905

Woodkirk Station, *c.* 1905

Woodkirk Station, August 1956.

Beeston Station, *c.* **1905.**

Main Stations in Bradford

* Originally named Bradford Drake Street until April 1867.

As noted elsewhere, for a town of such commercial importance railways arrived relatively late in Bradford, partly because several lines bypassed the town on their way to Leeds and also because disputes between companies delayed construction. The first station in the town was on the Leeds & Bradford Railway, opening on 1 July 1846 as a terminus situated in the vicinity of Market Street, after which it was named (at least according to some sources). The line serving it ran from Shipley and formed a short spur off the Leeds — Skipton route. The Leeds & Bradford Railway had been leased to the Midland Railway from the day Market Street Station opened and was eventually absorbed entirely from 4 October 1852. It was rebuilt and extended in the following year but operating requirements outstripped capacity and the enlarged Market Street was closed from 2 March 1890 when a new station was brought into use. The new station was officially renamed Forster Square by the London Midland & Scottish from 2 June 1924.

The Leeds & Bradford had been propelled into the hands of George Hudson and the Midland Railway after a rift with its erstwhile ally, the Manchester & Leeds Railway. This dispute was to have a permanent effect on the railways in Bradford since it led to the creation of two termini, Forster Square and Exchange, divided by around 300 yards of the town centre and thus depriving it of a main through station. Exchange was the second station in the town, being constructed by the Lancashire & Yorkshire, as successor to the Manchester & Leeds, and opened on 9 May 1850.

Bradford's third station, another terminus, opened on 1 June 1855 with the line of the Leeds, Bradford & Halifax Junction Railway, which two years before had been gathered into the fold of the Great Northern Railway. The opening of Adolphus Street, as the new station was known, had been delayed several months after the partial collapse of its overall roof. This may have been an ill omen, since hardly had trains started using it than some of the LB&HJR's directors began voicing complaints that it was inconveniently sited for the centre of town – which was true – and that matters would improve only if a connection could be made to the Lancashire & Yorkshire line into Exchange. It took until 1864 to obtain parliamentary approval for a spur from Hammerton Street Junction on the LB&HJR to Mill Lane Junction on the Lancashire & Yorkshire, and when it opened for passenger traffic on 7 January 1867 Adolphus Street was closed to passengers and became a goods station, in which capacity it served the Great Northern and its successors until the 1970s.

Exchange Station became the joint property of the Lancashire & Yorkshire and the Great Northern, who enlarged it in 1880 to a grand structure of ten platforms. It passed into the joint ownership of the London Midland & Scottish and London & North Eastern at the Grouping in 1923 and remained the main terminus for traffic from Kings Cross, including Pullman trains, until the 1980s. However, reductions in the West Riding's passenger network meant that it was deemed too large by the post-Beeching era and in 1973 it was officially closed and replaced by a new, smaller, station 200 or so yards further south. In 1977 a new bus station was opened next door and Exchange was renamed Bradford Interchange in 1983. In 1992 Forster Square became the terminus for intercity main line services.

Bradford Market Street, *c.* 1906.

Exterior of Bradford Market Street, *c.* 1908.

Bradford Market Street, *c.* 1905.

Main Stations in Bradford

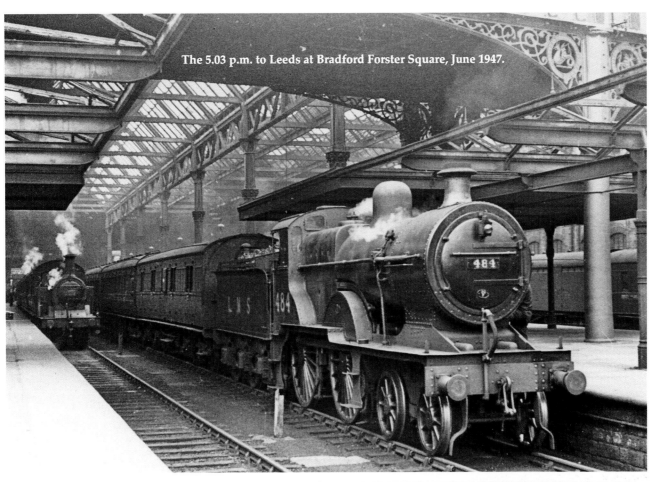

The 5.03 p.m. to Leeds at Bradford Forster Square, June 1947.

Bradford Forster Square, April 1949. In 1990 the old station was closed and a new smaller station built immediately to the west of the old one.

Main Stations in Bradford

Bradford Forster Square, April 1949.

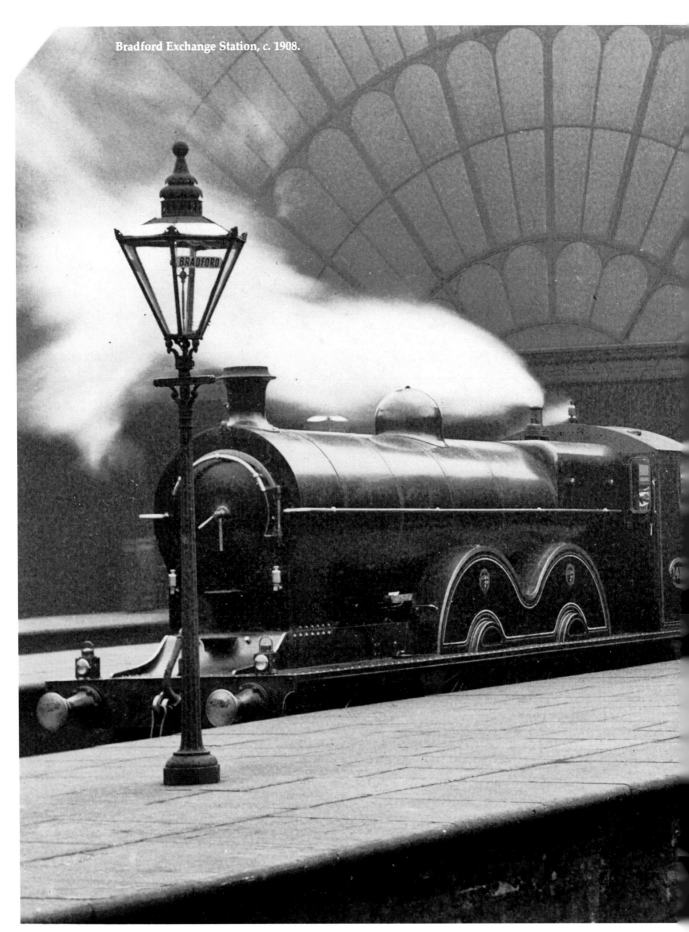

Bradford Exchange Station, *c.* 1908.

EXCHANGE
STATION BF

Bradford Exchange Station, *c.* 1908.

Bradford Exchange Station.

Main Stations in Bradford

Bradford — Queensbury

Passenger service withdrawn	23 May 1955
Distance	4 ¹/₂ miles
Company	Great Northern Railway

Stations closed	*Date of closure*
St Dunstan's	15 September 1952
Manchester Road	31 December 1915
Horton Park	15 September 1952
Great Horton	23 May 1955
Clayton	23 May 1955

This section of railway was the link between Bradford and Queensbury, originally planned to go beyond the latter to Thornton, on the route which eventually reached Keighley. Planned in 1872, it was taken over in the early stages by the Great Northern which in due course built the line. Construction began in 1874 and the line opened for goods traffic as far as Clayton in August 1877. The tunnel beyond Clayton, over 1,000 yards long, delayed passenger services to Thornton until October of the following year, trains running from Bradford Manchester Road and calling at Great Horton and Clayton. In November St Dunstan's Station opened, followed by Horton Park two years later – this becoming the most convenient for Park Avenue cricket and football grounds.

The fortunes of this line were for most of its life entwined with those of the Halifax — Keighley route and suffered a similar fate at the hands of competing road bus and tram services. An early casualty was Manchester Road Station, closing during the Great War, while St Dunstan's and Horton Park followed in 1952, three years before passenger services over the lines through Queensbury ended completely. It was argued at the time that closure would save £49,000 a year, a considerable sum equivalent to many times that figure today. Goods services continued until the line closed entirely beyond Horton Park in 1972.

The signal box at St Dunstan's.

A local train passing Horton Park Junction.

Great Horton Station, 1904.

GT HORTON STATION

Clayton Station facing Queensbury, April 1954 .

Bradford — Shipley

Passenger service withdrawn	2 February 1931
Distance	8 $\frac{1}{4}$ miles
Company	Bradford, Eccleshill & Idle Railway
	Idle & Shipley Railway

Stations closed	*Date of closure*
Eccleshill	2 February 1931
Idle	2 February 1931
Thackley	2 February 1931
Shipley & Windhill *	2 February 1931

* Originally named Shipley until 1 July 1887.

This short line, only six and a quarter miles long from its junction with the Bradford — Leeds route at Laisterdyke, was originally promoted by two local companies, the Bradford, Eccleshill & Idle Railway, which received its Act of incorporation in 1866 and the Idle & Shipley Railway, authorised a year later. Neither could raise sufficient capital to pursue its objects, so the Great Northern, seeing an opportunity to expand its influence, stepped in. Obtaining control in 1871, the Great Northern completed the double track line four years later.

Despite the existence of a connection onto the Midland Railway, the line ran into its own station at Shipley because the Midland opposed the use of its more conveniently located station on the line to Skipton. The Midland offered a quicker service to Bradford and the Great Northern line's passenger traffic suffered accordingly, though the company offered up to ten return journeys daily. Goods traffic, including stone from a quarry near Idle was always a more important source of revenue and this long outlived the passenger services which the London & North Eastern, as successors to the Great Northern, withdrew in 1931. The line also offered a route for express goods services between Bradford and Manchester which lasted into the 1960s, but in 1964 the line was closed between Laisterdyke and Idle. Final closure of the remainder followed in 1968.

Thackley Station, *c.* 1912.

Shipley Windhill Station from the dead end, September 1953.

Shipley Windhill facing the dead end, September 1953.
The connection to the Midland Railway on the right.

Bradford — Wakefield via Morley

Passenger service withdrawn	See text
Distance	14 miles
Company	Leeds, Bradford & Halifax Railway

Stations closed	*Date of closure*
St Dunstan's	15 September 1952
Laister Dyke	4 July 1966
Dudley Hill (first station) *	1 October 1875
Dudley Hill (second station)	7 April 1952
Birkenshaw & Tong	5 October 1953
Drightlington **	1 January 1962
Gildersome West ***	13 June 1955
Morley Top ****	2 January 1961
Tingley	1 February 1954
Ardsley	2 November 1964

* Replaced by the second station 605 metres north.
** Originally named Drightlington & Adwalton until 12 June 1961.
*** Originally named Gildersome until 2 March 1951.
**** Originally named Morley until 2 March 1951.

This section of line was built in two parts, the first – as far as Gildersome – being initially for coal traffic, though opening in August 1856 for passengers as well. Before this, in 1854, it was decided to extend the line to Wakefield and this section opened to traffic in October 1857. Two months later a Bradford — London direct service began, operated by the Great Northern. Local traffic was handled by the Leeds, Bradford & Halifax Junction Railway to begin with but in 1865 it was incorporated into the Great Northern. Through services to London became a regular feature of the line for much of its existence, though local traffic was not as brisk as had been anticipated, particularly when the Bradford — Wakefield line via Batley opened.

Duplication of routes between Bradford and Wakefield saw the demise of the stopping services on the line through Morley at the time of the introduction of multiple-unit diesel trains in 1957. Expresses continued for a time, but were withdrawn in 1966. The final section through Laisterdyke and Dudley Hill followed in 1981, to date the last closure on Great Northern's West Riding network.

St Dunstan's Station.

Birkenshaw and Tong Station, *c.* 1925.

Ardsley Station, 1912.

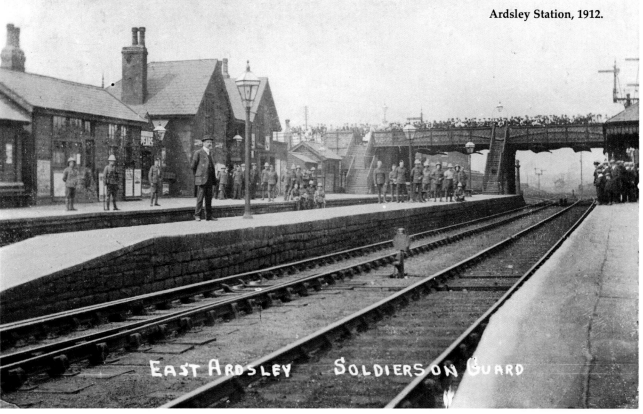

Bradley — Leeds: The Leeds New Line

Passenger service withdrawn	5 October 1953
Distance	14 ¹/₄ miles
Company	London & North Western Railway

Stations closed	*Date of closure*
Battyeford *	5 October 1953
Northorpe Higher **	5 October 1953
Heckmondwike Spen ***	5 October 1953
Liversedge Spen ***	5 October 1953
Cleckheaton Spen ***	5 January 1953
Gomersal	5 October 1953
Birstall Town ****	1 August 1951
Gildersome *****	11 July 1921
Farnley & Wortley †	3 November 1952

* Originally named Battyeford & Mirfield until 2 May 1910.
** Originally named Northorpe until 2 June 1924.
*** The suffix 'Spen' was added to the original names on 2 June 1924.
**** Originally named Upper Birstal until renamed as Upper Birstall on 1 April 1907. Renamed Birstall Town on 8 July 1935.
***** Closed between 1 August 1917 and 5 May 1919. Become a goods station and renamed Gildersome East from March 1951.
† Originally named Wortley & Farnley until 1 April 1891.

Gomersal Station, 1905.

One of the problems of the railway age during the nineteenth century was that successful routes often struggled to keep abreast in the growth of traffic – a situation reversed in the twentieth century, but reversed again in the twenty-first in an increasing number of places. Thus it was that by the 1880s the London & North Western was becoming concerned at the congestion on its existing route from Manchester to Leeds and saw a solution in building a 14 ¼ mile line from Heaton Lodge to Wortley; unsurprisingly, this became known as the Leeds New Line. This route duplicated some parts of the Lancashire & Yorkshire's Spen Valley Line, though in the latter part of the nineteenth century there was enough business in districts like the West Riding to satisfy everyone.

The New Line was far from easy to construct – the earlier routes had taken the more favourable terrain – and involved a tunnel one mile and 379 yards long at Gildersome, as well as a number of large viaducts and climbs in both directions to the summit at Birstall. The Heaton Lodge — Northorpe section opened to goods in September 1899 and the remainder eleven months later, passenger services starting in October 1900. The passenger services were local in character, longer distance expresses using the original line; as so often in these cases, the route was mainly useful for goods traffic, which could be kept separate from the faster trains. Thus, the line was seen as a duplicate for existing routes and passenger traffic ceased in 1953, though Gildersome had lost its passenger trains as early as 1921. In later years some through passenger services were routed over the line, but by 1965 these had all been diverted away and the line was closed from Farnley to Liversedge. The rump of the line served an oil terminal at Liversedge until 1986 when it closed completely.

Bramley — Pudsey & Dudley Hill

Passenger service withdrawn	15 June 1964
Distance	4 $^1/_2$ miles
Company	Great Northern Railway

Stations closed	*Date of closure*
Pudsey Lowtown	15 June 1964
Pudsey Greenside	15 June 1964
Dudley Hill (first station) *	1 October 1875
Dudley Hill (second station)	7 April 1952

* Replaced by the second station 605 metres north.

Though very close to Leeds, the manufacturing town of Pudsey was without rail connections until 1877 when the Great Northern opened a short single-track branch from Stanningley, on the direct Leeds — Bradford line to Greenside, passenger services starting a year later. The line generated sufficient traffic to justify doubling the track and building a short extension to Tyersal in 1893, where a triangular junction allowed through running northward to Laisterdyke and Bradford and southward to join the Lancashire & Yorkshire at Low Moor. The description of the line from Batley to Leeds via Tingley (see separate section) outlined the joint Great Northern and Lancashire & Yorkshire circular service, which used part of this extension; though the circular service ended in 1914, and the Dudley Hill to Low Moor section lost its passenger trains altogether. The Pudsey loop prospered far better, twenty return journeys using it daily after the Second World War, but afterwards its fortunes declined. It fell foul of the Beeching Report's dislike of duplicating routes and saw its last passenger trains on 15 June 1964; goods traffic lasted a matter of weeks longer.

Pudsey Greenside Station, August 1921.

Pudsey Low Town Station.

Brockholes — Holmfirth

Passenger service withdrawn	2 November 1959
Distance	1 ³/₄ miles
Company	Huddersfield & Sheffield Junction Railway

Stations closed	*Date of closure*
Thongs Bridge *	2 November 1959
Holmfirth *	2 November 1959

* Closed between 3 December 1865 and 11 March 1867.

Many early railways were constructed along the easiest available routes, primarily as through routes linking main centres of population and trade. In so doing they often bypassed smaller towns, or else, as with the line to Holmfirth, connecting them to the main line by short branches. Thus it was that Holmfirth's railway opened in July 1850 as an integral part of the Huddersfield & Sheffield Junction Railway's line between Huddersfield and Penistone. There were originally plans to extend the line to Holmbridge, two miles beyond Holmfirth; and even more ambitious schemes to reach the Manchester, Sheffield & Lincolnshire Railway at Crowden on the Woodhead route, or the Midland Railway at Hathersage. These all came to nothing, though the line was built as double track throughout. The line was worked from the outset by the Lancashire & Yorkshire Railway, which in due course absorbed it and the main line of the Huddersfield & Sheffield.

The Lancashire & Yorkshire did not have an untroubled ownership of the line, having to replace an original wooden trestle viaduct at Mytholmbridge with a similar structure, which itself required replacement with one of stone construction. The latter managed to collapse over part of its length in 1865 and the line was closed until 1867 for repairs. Passenger services were operated from Bradford and lasted into the British Railways era, ending in 1959 despite public protests. Occasional passenger excursions used the line for a further six years, when all services were ended and the line closed completely.

Thongsbridge Station, *c.* 1910.

THONGSBRIDGE STATION.

Thongsbridge Station, August 1953.

Holmfirth Station, *c.* **1910.**

Locomotive No. 42409 with the 5.05 p.m. to Bradford at Holmfirth, August 1953.

Holmfirth Station, August 1953.

Castleford — Garforth

Passenger service withdrawn   22 January 1951
Distance   7 miles
Company   North Eastern Railway

Stations closed	*Date of closure*
Ledston *	22 January 1951
Bowers Halt	22 January 1951
Kippax	22 January 1951

* Originally named Ledstone until 1 July 1915.

This was originally planned as part of the route of the Leeds, Castleford & Pontefract Junction Railway, a line promoted as a result of dissatisfaction with the North Eastern Railway in 1872 but ironically then rescued and partly constructed by that company three years later. The North Eastern decided to institute a passenger service over the line, which had originally been intended for goods alone, and by 1910 the trains connected Leeds and Pontefract by means of a new connection at Cutsyke. A third intermediate station at Bowers was opened by the London & North Eastern soon after the Grouping, but by 1946 the train service comprised only five return journeys daily. The zeal of the Railway Executive in pruning unremunerative services spelt the doom of the passenger service in 1951, though the line continued in use for coal traffic until the 1990s.

Kippax Station, *c.* 1905.

Kippax Station, *c.* 1905.

Dewsbury — Wakefield

Passenger service withdrawn	1 December 1930
Distance	1 $\frac{1}{2}$ miles
Company	Lancashire & Yorkshire Railway

Stations closed	*Date of closure*
Dewsbury Market Place *	1 December 1930

* Originally named Dewsbury until 2 June 1924.

Dewsbury was for many years the centre of the trade in 'shoddy', a coarsely woven cloth produced from waste wool, and this commercial prominence made it an attractive proposition for railway promoters. The West Riding Union Railway had originally planned a line to Dewsbury in 1851 but when the company became part of the Lancashire & Yorkshire they abandoned the project. However, the threat of competition from the London & North Western and the Great Northern caused the Lancashire & Yorkshire to reconsider the scheme and in 1861 it received Parliamentary approval for a very short branch to Dewsbury off the Calder Valley line between Horbury and Ravensthorpe. A triangular junction was later created by adding a third line diverging westward off the branch at Thornhill. Construction was leisurely, the line being more or less complete by 1866 and opened to passengers in April of the following year.

An ample passenger service of up to nineteen return journeys daily was initially provided but this was curtailed in the early years of the twentieth century. The London, Midland & Scottish Railway decided the line was a suitable candidate to lose its passenger services when the Great Depression cast its shadow over the country and the last train ran on 1 December 1930. Goods services ran into the 1950s, closing finally in 1961 apart from a half-mile section of line from the junction which still survives.

Copley Station, *c*. 1905.

Goole — Selby

Passenger service withdrawn	15 June 1964
Distance	12 miles
Company	North Eastern Railway

Stations closed	*Date of closure*
Airmyn *	15 June 1964
Drax **	15 June 1964
Barlow	15 June 1964

* Originally named Airmyn & Rawcliffe until 12 June 1961.
** Originally named Drax Hales until 12 June 1961.

The port of Goole, situated twenty miles west of Hull on the Yorkshire Ouse, was an early objective of railway builders. Considering the dominance of the North Eastern Railway and its constituents in the East Riding it is paradoxical that the first line to Goole was opened in March 1848 by the Lancashire & Yorkshire Railway, a company which had few other lines in that part of the county although it did gain running powers into Hull over the North Eastern in 1863.

A line from Selby to Goole had been projected by the York & North Midland in the period of the 'Railway Mania' of the 1840s, but the bubble of speculation burst before anything could come of it and it was not until 1903 that the North Eastern got round to constructing a short connection between the Leeds — Selby line and Goole, the junction being at Thorpe Willoughby.

Apart from ease of access to Goole, the line seems to have generated little passenger traffic and for much of the twentieth century had a service of only three return journeys a day. During the inter-war years the London & North Eastern attempted to develop traffic further by using Sentinel steam railcars, but this does not seem to have had any lasting effect. In later London & North Eastern and British Railways days it was operated by steam push-pull trains and latterly by multiple-unit diesel sets. Nevertheless, the route remained in use until the mid 1960s when it closed as part of the rationalisation of lines in the area.

Airmyn and Rawcliffe Station facing towards Goole, August 1956.

Drax Hales Station.

Barlow Station facing towards Goole, August 1956.

Greetland — Stainland

Passenger service withdrawn	23 September 1929
Distance	1 $^3/_4$ miles
Company	Lancashire & Yorkshire Railway

Stations closed	Date of closure
Greetland *	10 September 1962
West Vale	23 September 1929
Stainland & Holywell Green	23 September 1929

* Originally named North Dean until 1 January 1883 when it was renamed
Greetland & North Dean. Renamed again on 1 January 1897.

Unlike the line from Sowerby Bridge to Rishworth this very short branch was not originally conceived as part of a much longer route, but nevertheless boasted a series of large and expensive earthworks and structures, including two viaducts with 27 arches between them, and was double track throughout. The main traffic was generated by several woollen mills, though passenger services began in January 1875 with goods following in September. It had been authorised by the same Act as the Rishworth branch, in 1865, so construction was slow, even allowing for the scale of the works.

Like the Rishworth line, the Lancashire & Yorkshire pinned its faith in the steam railmotor as a source of passenger traffic from 1907, but this could not stem the tide of competition from road transport after electric trams reached Stainland in 1921. Closure to passengers came in 1929, goods traffic outliving it by thirty years, finally ending in 1959.

Greetland Station facing east, April 1954.

West Vale Station, *c.* **1905.**

West Vale Station, *c.* **1905.**

Stainland and Holywell Green Station.

Stainland and Holywell Green Station.

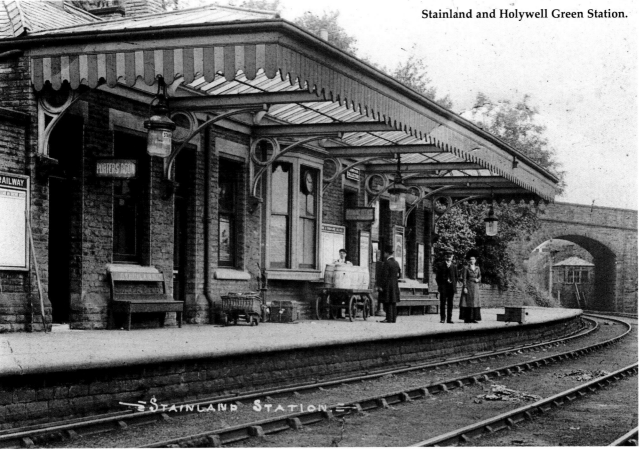

Greenfield — Delph

Passenger service withdrawn	2 May 1955
Distance	2 $^1/_2$ miles
Company	Lancashire & Yorkshire Railway

Stations closed	*Date of closure*
Moorgate	2 May 1955
Dobcross	2 May 1955
Measurements Halt	2 May 1955
Delph	2 May 1955

The Huddersfield & Manchester Railway & Canal Company had gained parliamentary approval for a line linking Cooper Bridge and Stalybridge in 1845, but before it opened in July 1849 it had been acquired by the London & North Western Railway, itself only recently created. The line passed through Saddleworth on its way north and thereby just missed the mill town of Delph. Local interests mobilised to persuade the company to construct a branch to Delph from a junction about half a mile north of Greenfield station. The line was completed by July 1851 and opened on 1 September in that year, a service of four trains daily being recorded in 1854. Two years later branch trains began operating to and from Oldham, seven trains daily in each direction being operated by 1879.

The passenger service on the line, which soon earned the nickname 'the Delph Donkey', possibly borrowed from a previous road carriage, was originally operated by a conventional locomotive and carriages. In 1910 the London & North Western began operating the line using steam railmotors, self-contained vehicles combining a small steam locomotive with a passenger carriage, which had the advantage of being able to be driven from either end. This sort of economy was being practiced by a number of companies at the time, as they were concerned at the relatively high costs of local train services, particularly in urban areas where competition from road transport was increasing. Though the railmotors were relatively short-lived, they were often succeeded by 'push-pull' trains and this was the method of passenger operation on the Delph line from the period of the Great War until closure.

Although the inter-war years and the Great Depression were a time of straitened circumstances for many secondary lines, the Delph branch managed to survive; indeed it acquired a new station – or rather a halt – from 18 March 1932 when Measurements Halt was opened between Dobcross and the terminus. It was created to serve the needs of workers at an adjacent factory – hence its name – and had a limited service apart from those necessary to convey employees. After the 1939 – 45 war, the future for small urban branches was considerably less promising; long-standing industries were in decline and road bus services took away passengers. The Delph Donkey made its last journey on 2 May 1955, considerably before the dawn of the Beeching era. The goods service continued until 4 November 1963 when coal traffic to Mallalieu's Bailey Mill at Delph ceased. There was a short-lived attempt to reopen at least a section in the early 1970s as a heritage line, but this came to nothing. Much of the route survives as a footpath.

Delph Station, c. 1950.

Halifax — Keighley

Passenger service withdrawn	23 May 1955
Distance	14 miles
Company	Great Northern Railway /
	Halifax & Ovenden Junction Railway
	(Great Northern & Lancashire & Yorkshire railways)

Stations closed	*Date of closure*
North Bridge *	23 May 1955
Ovenden *	23 May 1955
Holmfield *	23 May 1955
Queensbury	23 May 1955
Thornton	23 May 1955
Denholme	23 May 1955
Wilsden	23 May 1955
Cullingworth	23 May 1955
Ingrow East **	23 May 1955

* These stations were also on the Halifax & Ovenden Junction line.
** Originally named Ingrow until 2 March 1951.

From the 1860s the Great Northern Railway made strenuous efforts to expand its network into the West Riding, spending an estimated £1 million in building lines to serve the towns and industries of the area. A little over a century later the greater part of this network of railways had been closed completely, leaving behind a varied legacy of earthworks, tunnels and viaducts.

One of the centres of the Great Northern's lines was the town of Queensbury, north of Halifax, made famous in recent times by the Black Dyke Mills brass band. Here a trio of lines converged on a station built within a triangular junction with continuous platforms, an arrangement found in Britain only there and at Ambergate in Derbyshire. The first of the lines to Queensbury had started from Halifax, promoted in 1864 as the Halifax & Ovenden Junction Railway. The H&OJR was supported jointly by the Great Northern and the Lancashire & Yorkshire companies, who were obliged to take over responsibility for construction in 1870. By the middle of the nineteenth century Halifax was a populous town and the railway could only be made by demolishing a significant number of buildings along the route. The rising level of the land and the steep-sided valleys which cut through it made construction very difficult and costly and it was 1879 before the first passenger trains ran to Holmfield.

In the meantime a line was being constructed between Bradford and Thornton via Queensbury, with a connection southwards from there to the H&OJR at Holmfield and a further northward extension to Keighley. The Great Northern was not initially the promoter, but sensed its chance to develop its influence by taking over the ventures in 1872. Two years later work was under way on the Bradford — Thornton section and on a massive tunnel one mile, 741 yards in length south of Queensbury on the way to Holmfield. When opened with the line to Halifax four years later it was the longest on the Great Northern.

The line from Thornton to Keighley was also a major piece of construction, involving eight tunnels, including Lees Moor at 1,533 yards long, and two significant viaducts, one at Hewenden with seventeen arches and another at Cullingworth. Opening was staggered through 1884, the line as far as Denholme seeing its first traffic in January, the section to Ingrow following in March and the final section to Keighley, where trains ran into the Midland station, in November.

The lines converging on Queensbury were thus eventually completed only a few decades before electric street tramways began eroding away the railways' traffic. Trams from Bradford and Halifax reached Queensbury in 1900, but passenger services were retained until May 1955 when they eventually ceased. Goods traffic continued until the early 1970s, after which the track was lifted and the trackbed put to other uses. Little now remains, though the viaducts at Cullingworth, Hewenden, Thornton and Wheatley still remain as testimony to the Great Northern's efforts to build the lines through such difficult terrain.

North Bridge Halifax, April 1954.

Ovenden Station, c. 1910.

Queensbury Station.

Thornton Station facing
Keighley, April 1954.

Denholm Station, *c.* **1908.**

Denholme Station facing Keighley, April 1954.

Wilsden Station, *c.* 1905.

Hewenden Viaduct, near Wilsden.

WILSDEN VIADUCT   W. SERIES.

Cullingworth Station, *c.* **1900.**

Cullingworth Station looking towards Keighley, *c.* **1900.**

Ingrow East facing Queensbury, April 1954.

Holmfield — Halifax St Paul's

Passenger service withdrawn	1 January 1917
Distance	2 ¹/₂ miles
Company	Halifax High Level Railway

Stations closed	*Date of closure*
Pellon	1 January 1917
Halifax St Paul's	1 January 1917

The creation of this short section of railway is an example of a line planned originally as a through route but which came to nothing, leaving only a truncated fragment of the original scheme. In 1884 a grandiose plan with an extravagant title – the Halifax High Level & North & South Junction Railway – was proposed as a new route for Midland expresses between London and Scotland. The Hull & Barnsley's extension to Huddersfield would give access to a new high level station in Halifax, from whence trains would travel to Keighley over the Great Northern and then onto the Settle — Carlisle line. The Hull & Barnsley never got to Huddersfield and the scheme collapsed, leaving only a short section diverging from the Queensbury — Halifax line at Holmfield to the outer edges of Halifax, mainly to carry coal to the burgeoning mills of the area. The 2 ¹/₂ miles actually built included a tunnel of almost half a mile through solid rock, a ten-arch viaduct and a ruling gradient between 1 in 50 and 1 in 35 over parts of the route.

The line eventually opened in 1890, being jointly operated by the Great Northern, which ran all the passenger trains, and the Lancashire & Yorkshire; in 1894 the two companies became joint owners. The passenger service soon encountered stiff competition from the electric street tramway and was suspended in 1917 as a wartime economy, never to be reinstated. Goods services continued for much longer, finally ending in 1960.

Halifax St Pauls Station facing the dead end, September 1955.

Huddersfield — Kirkburton

Passenger service withdrawn	28 July 1930
Distance	4 ½ miles
Company	London & North Western Railway

Stations closed	*Date of closure*
Deighton	28 July 1930
Kirkheaton	28 July 1930
Fenay Bridge & Lepton *	28 July 1930
Kirkburton	28 July 1930

* Originally named Fenay Bridge until 1 September 1897.

The London & North Western Railway's line to Kirkburton was a further example of a plan for a through route which came to nothing, leaving only a short branch over part of the route. In this case the London & North Western was aiming to connect Huddersfield with Barnsley, though the latter end of the route was intended to be by running powers over other companies' lines. Unfortunately the other companies, the Midland and later the Hull & Barnsley, did not build the lines the London & North Western hoped for and so the Kirkburton branch remained a short but heavily engineered section of railway, laid out for double track and involving some significant earthworks, including two viaducts.

The first train to Kirkburton ran from Huddersfield on 6 October 1867, construction having occupied the previous two years. Originally there was only a station at Kirkburton, though it was technically in the village of Highburton. Kirkheaton and Fenay Bridge were opened in the months following the start of services and Deighton was added in 1871. In time Deighton became the source of much of the line's traffic, a chemical works opening there in the latter years of the nineteenth century which became an important maker of explosives during the Great War. Other munitions, mainly hand grenades, were made at Fenay Bridge.

The passenger service on the line gained the nickname of the 'Kirkburton Dick' over the years, but it fell victim to the bus services which developed after the Great War. The Depression of 1929 caused the London, Midland & Scottish Railway, which had absorbed the London & North Western in 1923, to withdraw passenger services from a number of branches all over the country and Kirkburton saw its last scheduled service in July 1930. Excursion trains for local millworkers continued to run during industrial holidays until the outbreak of war in 1939 and even after the conflict the line saw a number of enthusiasts' 'specials'. Goods traffic soldiered on until 1965 when the line was closed completely beyond the connection to the chemical works at Deighton. Even this succumbed in 1971, though a new station at Deighton was opened on the main line in 1982. The route is largely intact and is used as a walking and cycle path.

London and North Western 0-6-2 tank engine with a train at Kirkheaton.

Keighley — Oxenhope

Passenger service withdrawn	1 January 1962 (see text)
Distance	4 ³/₄ miles
Company	Midland Railway

Stations closed	*Date of closure*
Ingrow *†	1 January 1962
Damems *	23 May 1949
Oakworth *	1 January 1962
Haworth *	1 January 1962
Oxenhope *	1 January 1962

* Reopened 29 June 1968 by the Keighley & Worth Valley Preservation Society.
† Named Ingrow West between 2 March 1951 and 12 June 1961.

In the age of railway building, local initiatives were often needed to secure the building of secondary lines to link places bypassed by the main lines to the national network. Promoting and building a railway was one thing, but operating it was usually beyond the resources and abilities of local managements so it was often at the point of opening that one of the larger companies undertook to work the line for a substantial share of the receipts. In the fullness of time the larger undertaking might buy out the local concern, the original promoters generally receiving only a fraction of their initial investment in settlement, though no doubt satisfied that they had secured the benefits of the railway age for their locality.

So it was that in 1861 a group of people from the Worth Valley, south of Keighley, approached the Midland Railway about a branch to the Aire Valley line. The Midland agreed to operate a line promoted locally as an independent undertaking and the Keighley & Worth Valley Railway obtained its Act of incorporation in the following year. As with so many lines in the West Riding, construction took some time and it was not until 15 April 1867 that trains began running to Oxenhope. The Midland operated the line from the outset and bought it completely in 1881.

The Midland made considerable efforts to provide a comprehensive service, running eighteen return journeys in the years before the Great War. Despite competition from road transport there were still eight return journeys in the 1950s, but British Railways were by then trying to divest themselves of the line. It was proposed for closure in 1959, but this was turned down and multiple-unit diesel trains substituted for steam services. A further, and successful, application was made to close the line in 1961 and the last trains ran on 30 December.

However, the Worth Valley had not seen the end of its railway. In March 1962, encouraged by the success of the Bluebell Railway in Sussex, a society was formed to preserve the line as a steam-powered volunteer-operated undertaking. British Railways were unwilling to lease the route to the society and so it had to buy it outright. Train services resumed under the society's management in June 1968, at a time when railway enthusiasts from all over Britain and beyond were visiting the northwest to witness the final days of regular steam operation on British Railways and many called in on the Worth Valley at the same time. Two years later the line was used for the first feature film adaptation of Edith Nesbitt's *The Railway Children*, making the little railway famous. (By coincidence, the 1999 adaptation was filmed on the Bluebell line.) It continues to be one of Britain's premier steam railways and the society has succeeded in preserving the branch line character to a remarkable degree.

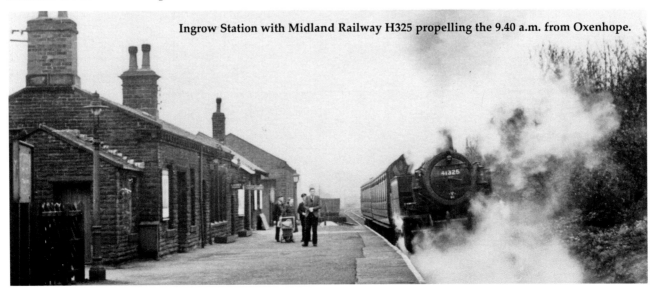

Ingrow Station with Midland Railway H325 propelling the 9.40 a.m. from Oxenhope.

Ingrow Station facing Oxenhope, May 1954.

Oakworth Station, *c.* 1900.

Haworth Station, 1905.

Oxenhope Station, 1906.

LMS Locomotive No. 1275 with the 1.15 p.m. from Keighley at Oxenhope Station, October 1946.

Knottingley — Askern Junction

Passenger service withdrawn	10 March 1947 *
Distance	10 miles
Company	Wakefield, Pontefract & Goole Railway

Stations closed	*Date of closure*
Womersley	10 March 1947
Norton	10 March 1947
Askern	10 March 1947

* This was the date of the last train; official closure was on 27 September 1948.

The Lancashire & Yorkshire Railway, in fulfilment of its title, operated across the West Riding and into the East, eventually reaching the port of Goole. In fact, the line to Goole opened early in the railway age and a connecting line from Knottingley struck out southeastwards to Askern Junction, where it connected eventually with the Great Northern Railway at Shaftholme Junction, its most northerly point on the East Coast main line. The Askern line opened in June 1848 and soon became a part of the east coast route, until the North Eastern built its line from York to Doncaster via Selby. Even so, the line through Askern remained a significant route for long distance trains including the Liverpool — Harwich cross-country boat trains, many of which were patronised by emigrants from northern Europe aiming to settle in the United States and Canada who wanted as direct a passage as possible across England. The London & North Eastern Railway later ran its 'North Country Continental' services over the line in the inter-war years, affording a connection between Harwich and York. The stopping trains on the line ended in the last year of the London & North Eastern; they were outlasted by the through workings which ceased on 11 July, just four months later. The route still survives, used by coal traffic.

Askern Station, *c.* 1908.

Main Stations in Leeds

Stations closed (with original owning company)	Date of closure
Leeds Hunslet Lane (Midland Railway)	1 March 1851
Leeds Wellington (first station) (Midland Railway) *	30 September 1850
Leeds Wellington (second station) (Midland Railway)	2 May 1938
Leeds New (London & North Western)	2 May 1938
Leeds Central (Manchester & Leeds Railway)	1 May 1967

* A temporary station replaced by the second station.

As railways developed in Britain they often outgrew their original facilities and in Leeds there has been a progressive expansion and later consolidation of main passenger stations. The original Leeds & Selby Railway station was situated at Marsh Lane and opened in 1834, but in 1846 the Midland, approaching from Rotherham, opened a more centrally located station off Wellington Street, known as Leeds Wellington.

In 1854 a second station was opened off Wellington Street, known as Leeds Central, and originally owned by the Manchester & Leeds Railway and the London & North Western, though initially the latter made considerable use of running powers into the Midland station at Wellington. Over the following fifteen years a series of proposals for new stations and improved traffic arrangements were proposed and opposed until in 1869 the North Eastern and London & North Western jointly opened a further station adjacent to the Midland at Wellington, this being Leeds New. This was of particular importance in allowing traffic from Manchester to run directly onto the North Eastern system in order to gain access to Newcastle, York, Selby and Hull. The Manchester & Leeds Railway had long since been absorbed by the Lancashire & Yorkshire, which made the most use of Central, the London & North Western showing a decided lack of interest in its part of the place. However, in the meantime the Great Northern had begun to use Central as its West Riding network expanded. The opening of the Settle — Carlisle route in 1876 meant that Midland trains, approaching from the southeast, now had to run past Wellington Station before reversing into it; though this was by no means a unique arrangement elsewhere in Britain, it was certainly an inconvenient one.

By 1913 Wellington was the Midland's preserve, while the London & North Western and North Eastern used both Leeds New and Central, the latter in the company of the Lancashire & Yorkshire and the Great Northern. The Grouping of 1923 consolidated ownership, Wellington being wholly owned by the London Midland & Scottish while Central and New were jointly owned by that company and the London & North Eastern. On 2 May 1938 Wellington and New stations were combined to become Leeds City, part of Wellington being turned over to goods traffic. Central continued in use into the British Railways era, but in 1967 it was closed and all its remaining traffic transferred to City, which had meanwhile been rebuilt in 1962 with the addition of a large office block. Paradoxically, by the 1990s City was deemed inadequate to cope with the volume of traffic using it and its capacity was extended in 2002.

Leeds Wellington Station, *c.* 1905.

LEEDS (WELLINGTON) STATION.

No. 242 with the 3.15 p.m. to Hellifield
at Leeds Wellington Station, June 1933.

Leeds New Station from the east, *c.* **1908.**

Leeds New Station from the west, *c.* **1908.**

Main Stations in Leeds

Lockwood — Meltham

Passenger service withdrawn	23 May 1949
Distance	3 ¹/₂ miles
Company	Lancashire & Yorkshire Railway

Stations closed	*Date of closure*
Woodfield	1 July 1874
Netherton	23 May 1949
Healey House	23 May 1949
Meltham Mills	September 1934
Meltham	23 May 1949

So many minor lines in the West Riding were constructed as part of ambitious plans which came to nothing, but the line to Meltham was intended for local traffic, particularly a thread mill in the town. The Lancashire & Yorkshire promoted the branch from Lockwood and construction began in 1864 on what should have been a straightforward piece of civil engineering. It was soon discovered that the soil and rock through which the line was to go were unstable and prone to landslips; this first postponed opening for goods traffic until August 1868 and then caused the line to be closed soon after until remedial works could be completed. Massive retaining walls produced the desired effect and passenger services began on 5 July 1869.

The 'Coddy', as the passenger service was known (a title shared with the other branch trains in the West Riding), provided a respectable service of up to eleven journeys a day in each direction. The closure of the thread mill in 1934 was a blow, but the use of the vacant buildings as a tractor factory led to considerable flows of traffic during the Second World War when it was turned over to producing engine components for aircraft and tanks. In the post-war period passenger traffic declined due to bus competition – the line was too far away from Huddersfield to have been affected by trams in the earlier years of the century – and 'the Coddy' ran for the last time in May 1949. Goods traffic ceased in 1965, though the tractor factory remained in production until the late 1980s.

Meltham Station, *c.* 1910.

Lofthouse — Methley

Passenger service withdrawn	2 November 1964
Distance	5 miles
Company	Methley Joint
	(Great Northern, Lancashire & Yorkshire and North Eastern)

Stations closed	*Date of closure*
Stanley	2 November 1964
Methley South *	7 March 1960

* Originally named Methley until 2 March 1951.

Despite the widespread Victorian belief in the virtues of competition, railway companies often saw the value of collaboration over certain projects, either to share their benefits or to limit the difficulties which might be caused by one company promoting a line into another's territory. The latter case is exemplified by the Methley Joint line, which was mainly the brainchild of the Great Northern striking out eastwards from its Bradford — Wakefield line to meet the Lancashire & Yorkshire and the North Eastern at Castleford. The latter two companies, initially opposed to the scheme, decided it was in their interest to combine with the Great Northern in a joint line, not least to ensure it extended no further. The line was authorised in 1864 and opened to goods traffic – mainly coal – the following year. Passenger services had to wait until 1 May 1869, though these were almost entirely provided by the Great Northern, its partners being content to rely on goods for revenue. In 1867 and 1868 the Great Northern offered a through service between Bradford and York over the Methley Joint, but it ceased thereafter.

The line crossed the floodplain of the Calder and flooding caused considerable difficulties over the years, a problem exacerbated by mining subsidence during the twentieth century. The local passenger service was good, though forward connections to Wakefield were only possible with a change at Ardsley. Methley boasted three stations, the Midland and the Lancashire & Yorkshire providing their own facilities; unsurprisingly the Methley Joint station closed in 1960 and the whole route's passenger and through goods services followed four years later. Colliery traffic kept fragments of the line in use until 1982.

Stanley Station.

Lofthouse North Junction — Stourton Junction

Passenger service withdrawn	1 October 1904
Distance	5 miles
Company	East & West Yorkshire Union Railway

Stations closed	*Date of closure*
Robin Hood	1 October 1904
Rothwell	1 October 1904
Stourton	1 October 1904

In the annals of short-lived passenger services, this five-mile stretch of line must rate as one of the prime examples as the East & West Yorkshire Union Railway saw regular passenger trains for only nine months. The line was conceived as a connection between the Hull & Barnsley at Drax and Leeds, that company promoting the other, notionally independent, company when its own plans for a line were brought to nothing by 1886. There had been a plan for an extension to serve collieries owned by the Charlesworth family and in the end this was all that was constructed, the line diverging from the Great Northern at Lofthouse and the Midland at Stourton.

Passenger trains commenced from 4 January 1904 using coaches hired from the Midland, but it was a vain attempt to compete with the developing electric street tramways and the service ceased before the year was out. In truth, coal was the motive for building the line and this provided its mainstay as long as it survived, closure coming in 1966 though the through route had been cut five years before. The only passenger trains to traverse the line for most of its life were excursions, heading for east coast resorts like Bridlington and Scarborough. The East & West Yorkshire Union Railway was absorbed by the London & North Eastern in 1923.

Marshland Junction — Fockerby *

Passenger service withdrawn	17 July 1933
Distance	10 miles
Company	Isle of Axholme Joint Railway
(jointly owned by the North Eastern and Lancashire & Yorkshire railways)	

Stations closed	*Date of closure*
Reedness Junction	17 July 1933
Eastoft	17 July 1933
Luddington	17 July 1933

* The closed station on this line that was in Lincolnshire was Fockerby; other stations on the IoAJR also in Lincolnshire were Crowle, Belton, Epworth, Haxey Town and Haxey Junction.

The Light Railways Act of 1896 was intended to allow remote areas with sparse populations to benefit from a railway by allowing for the construction of lines, either to standard or narrow gauges, which were more lightly engineered than major routes. Signalling and station facilities were simplified, speeds kept low, and instead of a costly Act of Parliament the project could be authorised by a Light Railway Order.

As related in *Lincolnshire's Lost Railways* the Isle of Axholme in northwest Lincolnshire was just the kind of area the 1896 Act was designed to help. The railway network was built by two companies, the Goole & Marshland and the Isle of Axholme Light. Between them they constructed a through route from Marshland Junction on the North Eastern Railway line from Goole to Doncaster to Haxey Junction on the Great Northern & Great Eastern Joint line from Doncaster to Lincoln. A line branched off eastwards from Reedness to near the Trent at Fockerby, with the intention of an extension to Scunthorpe, which was never built. The line's character as a light railway was revealed by the existence of an assortment of goods sidings, some public, others private, along the route – seventeen in all.

The line opened in stages between 1900 and 1909, but from 1 October 1902 the two light railways had been jointly acquired by the Lancashire & Yorkshire and North Eastern railways. Daily operation was largely in the hands of the Lancashire & Yorkshire and from the outset the main revenue came from goods, principally agricultural requisites and produce; peat cut from Hatfield Moor also contributed. The line passed into the joint ownership of the London Midland & Scottish and London & North Eastern railways at the Grouping in 1923 and attempts were made to economise on running costs, including the use of one of the new Sentinel-Cammell steam railcars. It was to no avail and the sparseness of the population and the general dearth of passengers led to the closure of all the passenger facilities in 1933, although the lines carried on with goods. The line south of Epworth closed in February 1956 and the rest of the line to Fockerby from 5 April 1965, though the section from Marshland Junction to Belton was retained until 1972 to serve the Central Electricity Generating Board power station at Keadby.

Saddleworth Station, *c.* 1906.

Skelmanthorpe Junction — Clayton West

Passenger service withdrawn	24 January 1983 (but see text)
Distance	3 ½ miles
Company	Lancashire & Yorkshire Railway

Stations closed	*Date of closure*
Skelmanthorpe	24 January 1983
Clayton West	24 January 1983

Clayton West is close to Barnsley and this was the attraction to the Lancashire & Yorkshire Railway in building a railway to the town from the Huddersfield — Penistone main line. The hope of extending to Barnsley or beyond preoccupied the company for much of the nineteenth century but nothing came of the schemes and the line remained a short branch for the whole of its existence.

Given that it was less than four miles long, the line took a long time to construct – work began in 1872 and it opened seven years later. Six return journeys satisfied passengers' needs, most trains running to and from Huddersfield, though some ran through to Bradford. Unlike many branches, goods traffic more or less succumbed to road competition before passenger traffic and the latter managed to go on well beyond the Beeching era of the 1960s, finally ending in 1983. The track remained for a further three years before being lifted.

This, however, was not so much the end of the line as a prelude to a new beginning. The standard gauge track was replaced by fifteen-inch metals, reopening at Clayton West in 1991 as the Kirklees Light Railway. By the following year the whole route had become a narrow gauge line, operated on weekends throughout the year and daily between May and September. The line may not have achieved the grandiose ambitions of the Lancashire & Yorkshire, but it has been carrying passengers almost continuously in three centuries.

Locomotive No. 44834 with the 4.10 p.m. from Huddersfield at Clayton West Station, April 1954.

Skelmanthorpe Station, *c.* 1906.

Skelmanthorpe Junction — Clayton West

Skelmanthorpe Junction — Clayton West

Sowerby Bridge — Rishworth

Passenger service withdrawn	8 July 1929
Distance	3 ³/₄ miles
Company	Lancashire & Yorkshire Railway

Stations closed	*Date of closure*
Watson's Crossing Halt	8 July 1929
Triangle	8 July 1929
Ripponden & Barkisland *	8 July 1929
Rishworth	8 July 1929

* Originally named Ripponden until 1 December 1891.

This short branch is a further example of a line originally planned as part of a much larger scheme which never came to fruition. In 1846 the Lancashire & Yorkshire Railway devised a plan for a more direct route between the West Riding and Lancashire which would avoid the existing steeply graded line through Summit Tunnel. Given the terrain, the new route was hardly going to be easy to construct and would have involved a four-mile tunnel under the Pennines at Blackstone Edge to reach Littleborough, which would have been the longest in the country at the time. Unsurprisingly, nothing was done at the time, railway construction being depressed after the end of the 'Railway Mania' of the 1840s.

Even so, the Lancashire & Yorkshire still harboured hopes of a more direct route westwards when it gained Parliamentary approval for a short branch line from Sowerby Bridge to Rishworth in 1865. A new station was opened at Sowerby Bridge eleven years later, ostensibly to serve the branch, but in all probability it was intended to be the junction for a new through route. The branch to Rishworth opened as far as Ripponden in 1878 and to Rishworth three years later, construction being delayed by the need for extensive tunnelling and other earthworks, as well as by landslips near Triangle. Built to main line standards the branch was destined never to go beyond Rishworth and the plan of an alternative route via Littleborough never materialised.

Such a short and heavily engineered line was unlikely to be particularly profitable, particularly after the rise of motor buses and trams. The Lancashire & Yorkshire provided a service of eleven return journeys daily, the passenger trains being known locally as 'the Rishworth Pig'. In 1907 the company used the branch, and the neighbouring one to Stainland, as the first lines on which to try their new steam railmotors and these eventually provided a service of eighteen return journeys daily. Despite such economies passenger services were withdrawn in 1929, three years after a bus service began to operate between Halifax and Rishworth. Goods traffic continued to Rishworth until 1952 when the line was closed beyond Ripponden; the foreshortened line struggled on a further six years, closing completely in 1958.

Watson's Crossing Halt.

Triangle Station, *c.* 1905.

Ripponden Station, *c.* 1910.

Thornhill — Low Moor: The Spen Valley Line

Passenger service withdrawn	14 June 1965
Distance	7 ¼ miles
Company	West Riding Union Railway

Stations closed	*Date of closure*
Ravensthorpe Lower *	30 June 1952
Heckmondwike **	14 June 1965
Liversedge **	14 June 1965
Cleckheaton **	14 June 1965

* Originally named Ravensthorpe until 30 September 1951.
** The names of these stations were suffixed 'Central' between 2 June 1924 and 12 June 1961.

The Lancashire & Yorkshire Railway gained access to Leeds as early as 1840 over a route originally constructed by the Manchester & Leeds Railway between those cities, and this route quickly became one of the main arteries of the West Riding's railway network. The line had followed the valley of the river Calder, so in the mid 1840s it seemed reasonable to construct a line along the valley of the river's tributary, the Spen, to offer a direct route between the Manchester & Leeds line and Bradford, taking in the growing towns of Heckmondwike, Liversedge and Cleckheaton along the way. The line was opened from Mirfield under the auspices of the West Riding Union Railway on 12 July 1848, though through services to Bradford had to wait a further two years until the section from Halifax through Low Moor was ready.

During the 1840s there had been a plan for the West Riding Union Railway to construct a connection between Thornhill on the Calder Valley line and Heckmondwike, allowing through running from Bradford to either Manchester or Barnsley. Powers had been allowed to lapse, though the land had been bought, and the Lancashire & Yorkshire, which by now had absorbed the West Riding Union, was uncertain whether to resurrect them. However, in 1861 it obtained new powers for the line, including a station at Ravensthorpe. Construction was at a leisurely pace, the route opening eventually in 1869.

The Spen Valley line gained further importance when running powers were granted to the Great Northern to use it, at least in part for the Huddersfield — Bradford circuit workings via Heckmondwike and Low Moor. The route was also used for excursions to east coast seaside resorts in season.

During the post-war era services declined, partly due to main line services being routed elsewhere, partly as a consequence of road competition. Multiple-unit diesel trains began in 1957, connecting Bradford and Huddersfield, but, as in many other places, modernisation came too late. The Beeching Report of 1963 recommended closure, which came for passengers two years later. Goods services succumbed during the 1970s, though small sections were retained for a time to serve local industries. Much of the route is now a cycleway.

Heckmondwike Station, *c.* **1905.**

Liversedge Station, the old station before it was rebuilt.

Liversedge Station, after it was rebuilt, *c.* 1904.

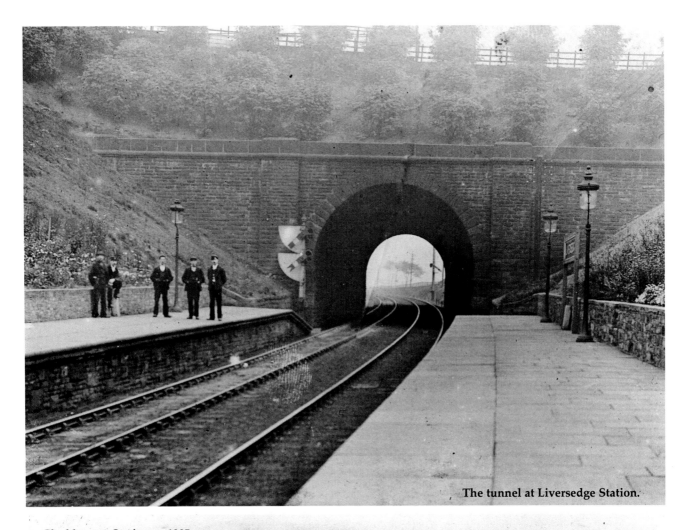

The tunnel at Liversedge Station.

Cleckheaton Station, *c.* 1905.

Wakefield — Drightlington via Batley

Passenger service withdrawn	7 September 1964
Distance	11 ¾ miles
Company	Bradford, Wakefield & Leeds Railway
	Leeds, Bradford & Halifax Junction Railway

Stations closed	*Date of closure*
Alverthorpe	5 April 1954
Flushdyke *	5 May 1941
Ossett	7 September 1964
Chickenley Heath	1 July 1909
Batley	7 September 1964
Upper Batley **	4 February 1952
Howden Clough	1 December 1952

* Originally named Ossett until 7 April 1864.
** Originally named Batley Upper (date of name change unknown).

This was another example of a line built in two sections by two companies aiming to connect with a place *en route*, in this case the mill town of Batley. From the south came the Bradford, Wakefield & Leeds Railway, which had already constructed its main line between those places, intent on reaching Batley via Ossett, which it did in April 1864, opening throughout to Batley by the end of the year. The Leeds, Bradford & Halifax Junction Railway had already completed its line between Bradford and Wakefield via Morley and started to construct a connection southwards from Drightlington & Adwalton. It reached Upper Batley in 1863, and Batley itself, where it made an end-on connection with the Bradford, Wakefield & Leeds, in 1864 – just in time for the Great Northern to scoop up the line into its growing West Riding empire in that year. In addition to the original stations at Flushdyke, Ossett and Batley, 1866 saw one opened at Howden Clough, Alverthorpe in 1872 and Chickenley Heath five years later.

As noted in the section dealing with the Bradford — Wakefield route via Morley, the line through Batley tended to take much of the local passenger traffic between those places while the Morley route was used for expresses. The original Bradford, Wakefield & Leeds section to Batley saw two of the Great Northern's steam railmotors, nos. 7 and 8, used for services from Ossett, starting on 19 February 1906, but they were not well received, lacking power for the rigours of the West Riding lines. Eventually they saw use over the whole line to Drightlington and also over the Batley — Ardsley and Ossett — Dewsbury routes, but their sojourn was brief and they had gone by October 1908, transferred to the less taxing metals of Lincolnshire. The writing was clearly on the wall for Chickenley Heath Station, which closed in July of the following year.

Passenger services were to continue until 1964, but throughout the 1950s there had been a slow progression of station closures so that by the end only Batley and Ossett remained. Goods services to Batley ceased from 5 May 1969 and little of the route still remains.

Chickenley Heath, September 1953.

A Great Northern Railway 0-4-2 locomotive at Batley Station with a passenger train, 1905.

Wakefield — Drightlington via Batley 73

Batley Station, September 1953.

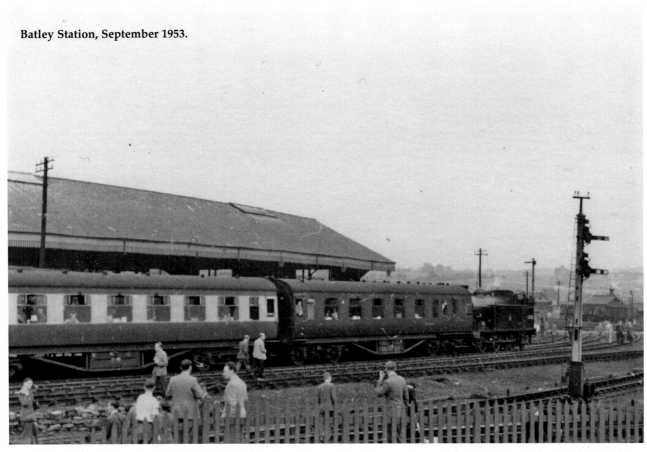

Upper Batley, *c.* **1900.**

Wyke — Cooper Bridge

Passenger service withdrawn	14 September 1931
Distance	3 ³/₄ miles
Company	Lancashire & Yorkshire Railway

Stations closed	*Date of closure*
Bailiff Bridge	2 April 1917
Clifton Road (Brighouse)	14 September 1931

This short section of railway was originally planned during the 1840s and sanctioned by Parliament in 1846 as part of the West Riding Union Railway, but when the company was absorbed into the Lancashire & Yorkshire in 1850 no work had been started and the company showed no inclination to rectify the situation. Powers lapsed and it was 1866 before the company undertook to construct a line southwards from Wyke Junction on the Bradford — Halifax route to Clifton Road, Brighouse. In 1875 further powers were obtained to join the branch to the Calder Valley line at Bradley Wood West Junction, so allowing through running from Bradford to Normanton and beyond. This was, in reality, the main purpose of the route and though a service of local trains was provided it ceased in 1931. By 1948 the through trains were re-routed away to use the Spen Valley line, partly because of fears about the state of Wyke Viaduct, the largest structure on the line, which was demolished in part during the 1970s. The route, which was in reality a cut-off rather than a branch, was often referred to as the Pickle Bridge branch, since Wyke Station had originally been named Pickle Bridge until 1882.

Baliff Bridge Station, *c.* **1905.**

Stanningley Station, *c.* **1904.**

Stations closed on lines still open to passengers
Bradford — Leeds

Stations closed	*Date*
Laister Dyke	**4 July 1966**
Stanningley *	**1 January 1968**
Armley Moor **	**4 July 1966**

* Named Stanningley for Farsley from an unknown date until 12 June 1961.
** Originally named Armley & Wortley until 25 September 1950.

Lancashire & Yorkshire Railway train on Great Northern rails at Stanningley, *c.* **1904.**

Armley & Wortley Station, *c.* **1905.**

Doncaster — Wakefield

* Originally named Adwick until renamed Adwick-le-Street & Carcroft in March 1867. Renamed Carcroft & Adwick-le-Street on 1 May 1880.

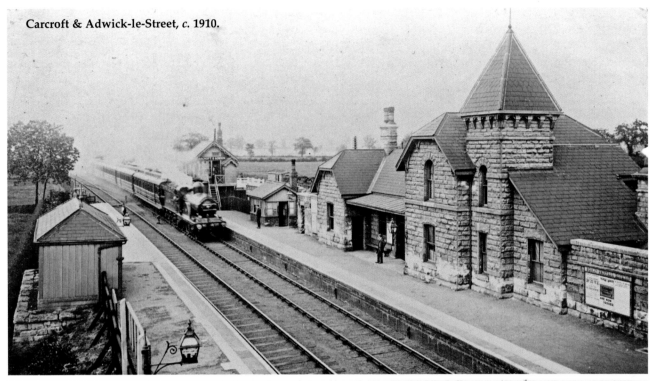

Carcroft & Adwick-le-Street, *c.* **1910.**

Hampole Station, *c.* **1904.**

HAMPOLE

An express approaching Hampole Station, *c.* **1904.**

Hemsworth Station, *c.* **1910.**

Hemsworth Station after widening in 1911/12.

East Coast main line: Retford — Doncaster — York *

Stations closed	Date
Bawtry **†	6 October 1958
Rossington **	6 October 1958
Doncaster (first station) ††	September 1850
Arksey **†††	5 August 1952
Moss	8 June 1953
Balne	15 September 1958
Heck	15 September 1958
Temple Hirst ††††	6 March 1961

* Closed stations on this line that were in Nottinghamshire were Barnby Moor & Sutton, Ranskill and Scrooby.
** Great Northern stations (the others were North Eastern).
† Official closure was after June 1965.
†† A temporary station replaced by the current Doncaster Station 400 metres south.
††† Originally named Stockbridge until renamed Arksey & Stockbridge in December 1850. Renamed again in September 1854.
†††† Originally named Temple Hurst; renamed by 1904.

Temple Hirst Station.

Halifax — Wakefield Kirkgate

Stations closed	Date
Halifax Shaw Syke	7 August 1850
Greetland *	10 September 1962
Elland (first station) **	1 August 1865
Elland (second station)	10 September 1962
Brighouse for Rastrick (first station) ***	1 May 1893
Cooper Bridge	20 February 1950
Mirfield (first station) ****	5 March 1866
Thornhill *****	1 January 1962
Horbury †	5 January 1970
Horbury Junction	11 July 1927

* Originally named North Dean until 1 January 1883 when it was renamed Greetland & North Dean. Renamed again on 1 January 1897.
** Replaced by the second station 185 metres west.
*** Replaced by the second station 300 metres east.
**** Replaced by the current Mirfield Station 185 metres east.
***** Originally named Dewsbury until January 1851.
† Named Horbury & Ossett between 25 March 1903 and 18 June 1962.

Cooper Bridge Station, *c*. 1905.

Thornhill Station, 1904.

Halifax — Wakefield Kirkgate

Horbury Junction, *c.* 1904.

Hebden Bridge — Burnley *

Stations closed	Date
Stansfield Hall	31 July 1944 **
Cornholme	26 September 1938
Portsmouth***	7 July 1958

* Closed stations on this line that were in Lancashire were Holme, Townsley and Burnley Manchester Road.
** This was the date of the last train; official closure was on 17 August 1949.
*** Before 1880 Portsmouth was in Lancashire; after that date the county boundry was reorganised placing the village in Yorkshire and to confuse matters British Railways renamed the station Portsmouth (Lancs).

Portsmouth Station, August 1921.

Huddersfield — Barnsley

Stations closed	Date
Berry Brow *	4 July 1966
Penistone Barnsley Road *	14 August 1916
Dodworth	29 June 1959
Summer Lane **	22 June 1959

* New Stations were opened in 1989.
* Closed between 1 December 1859 and 1 February 1867.

Berry Brow Station, c. 1904.

Berry Brow Station.

Knottingley — Swinton

Stations closed	Date
Ackworth *	2 July 1951
Frickley	8 June 1953
Swinton **	2 July 1899
Swinton Town ***	1 January 1968

* Official closure was after 21 July 1959.
** Originally named Swinton for Doncaster until 1853. Replaced by a second Swinton Station (see below) 185 metres due south.
*** Originally named Swinton until 25 September 1950. Officially closed on 7 September 1968.

Ackworth Station, 1905.

Leeds — Harrogate

Stations closed	Date
Arthington (first station) *	1 February 1865
Arthington (second station)	22 March 1965

* Originally named Pool until February 1852. Replaced by the second station 605 metres north.

Leeds — Hellifield

Stations closed	Date
Holbeck Low Level *	7 July 1958
Armley Canal Road **	22 March 1965
Kirkstall	22 March 1965
Kirkstall Forge	1 August 1905
Newlay ***	22 March 1965
Calverley & Rodley ****	22 March 1965
Apperley Bridge *****	22 March 1965
Thwaites	1 July 1909
Idle	1 October 1848
Keighley (first station) †	6 May 1883
Bingley (first station)	24 July 1892
Steeton & Silsdon (first station) ††	1 March 1892
Kildwick & Crosshills (first station)†††	7 April 1889
Kildwick & Crosshills (second station)	22 March 1965
Cononley	22 March 1965
Skipton (first station) ††††	30 April 1876
Bell Busk	4 May 1959
Hellifield (first station)	1 June 1880

* Originally named Holbeck until 2 March 1951.
** Originally named Armley until 25 September 1950.
*** Named Newlay for Horsforth between 1 April 1875 and 4 October 1889 and then Newlay & Horsforth until 12 June 1961.
**** Originally named Calverley until 1 October 1889.
***** Named Apperley from 1847 until 1 October 1890 and then Apperley & Rawdon until being renamed Apperley Bridge & Rawdon in May 1893. Reverted to its original name on 12 June 1961.
† Replaced by the current Keighley Station on the south side of the road bridge.
†† Originally named Steeton until 1 September 1868. Replaced by second station on opposite side of level crossing.
††† Originally named Kildwick until renamed Kildwick & Cross Hills on 1 January 1863; renamed again after 1 October 1884. Replaced by second station 320 metres west.
†††† Replaced by the current Skipton Station 200 metres north.

Kirkstall Station, *c.* 1905.

Newlay & Horsforth Station, *c.* 1907.

Calverley & Rodley Station, *c.* 1910.

Apperley Bridge & Rawdon Station, *c.* **1910.**

The original Bingley Station, which was closed in 1892.

Bell Busk Station, *c.* **1905.**

Leeds — Wakefield Kirkgate *

* Lancashire & Yorkshire Railway between Goose Hill Junction and Wakefield.
** Originally named Methley until 25 September 1950.

Manchester Victoria — Halifax & Bradford *

* Closed stations on this line that were in Lancashire were Miles Platting, Newton Heath and Middleton Junction.
** Replaced by the current Sowerby Bridge Station 605 metres west.
*** Closed between 1 January 1917 and 2 March 1919.

Luddendenfoot Station looking toward Manchester, April 1953.

Hipperholme Station, *c.* 1905.

Low Moor Station viewed from the east.

Manchester Victoria — Huddersfield — Leeds *

Stations closed	Date
Saddleworth	7 October 1968
Diggle	7 October 1968
Slaithwaite	7 October 1968
Golcar	7 October 1968
Longwood **	7 October 1968
Bradley (first station) ***	July 1849
Bradley (second station)	6 March 1950
Heaton Lodge	31 October 1864
Staincliffe & Batley Carr ****	7 April 1952
Churwell ****	2 December 1940
Farnley & Wortley †	3 November 1952

* Lancashire & Yorkshire Railway between Mirfield West Junction and Ravensthorpe and Stalybridge and Manchester Victoria. The closed station in Lancashire on this line was Clayton Bridge.
** Named Longwood & Milnsbridge between 1 July 1887 and 12 June 1961.
*** Replaced by the second station.
**** Closed between 1 January 1917 and 5 May 1919.
† Originally named Wortley & Farnley until 1 April 1891.

Saddleworth `Station, *c.* 1906.

Normanton — Leeds

Stations closed	Date
Altofts *	14 May 1990
Methley North **	16 September 1957
Hunslet (first station) ***	14 September 1873
Hunslet (second station)	13 June 1960

* Originally named Altofts & Whitwood until 4 May 1970.
** Originally named Methley until 25 September 1950.
*** Replaced by second station 505 metres north.

Selby — Leeds

Stations closed	Date
Hambleton	14 September 1959
Milford *	3 September 1904
Manston **	1 April 1869
Leeds Marsh Lane (first station) **	1 April 1869
Leeds Marsh Lane (second station)	15 September 1958

* Originally named Junction until renamed Milford Junction in December 1850. Renamed Milford from 1 May 1893.
** Closed between 9 November 1840 and November 1850. Replaced by the second station when the line was extended.

Sheffield — Wakefield

Stations closed	Date
Ecclesfield West *	6 November 1967
Wentworth & Hoyland Common **	2 November 1959
Haigh	13 September 1965
Crigglestone ***	13 September 1965
Horbury Junction	11 July 1927

* Originally named Ecclesfield until 25 September 1950.
** Originally named Wentworth & Tankersley until 1 July 1901.
*** Named Crigglestone West between 2 June 1924 and 12 June 1961.

Shipley — Bradford

Stations closed	Date
Shipley (first station) *	February 1875
Manningham	22 March 1965

* Replaced by the current Shipley Station 200 metres north.

Midland Railway trains passing each other at Manningham Station.

Swinton — York

* Originally named Ferrybridge until 1 June 1901.

Burton Salmon Station.

Monk Fryston Station, *c.* 1910.

Wakefield — Leeds

* Replaced by the current Wakefield Westgate Station.
** Originally named Holbeck until 2 March 1951.

Wakefield Westgate — Pontefract Monkhill